WALK THROUGH

A Field of Flowers

A collection of poems and short stories inspired by life, love, and some heartache along the way...

K.A. Bloch

BALBOA.PRESS

A DIVISION OF HAY HOUSE

This book is a work of non-fiction. Unless otherwise noted, the author and the publisher make no explicit guarantees as to the accuracy of the information contained in this book and in some cases, names of people and places have been altered to protect their privacy.

Balboa Press books may be ordered through booksellers or by contacting:

Balboa Press
A Division of Hay House
1663 Liberty Drive
Bloomington, IN 47403
www.balboapress.com
844-682-1282

Because of the dynamic nature of the Internet, any web addresses or links contained in this book may have changed since publication and may no longer be valid. The views expressed in this work are solely those of the author and do not necessarily reflect the views of the publisher, and the publisher hereby disclaims any responsibility for them.

The author of this book does not dispense medical advice or prescribe the use of any technique as a form of treatment for physical, emotional, or medical problems without the advice of a physician, either directly or indirectly. The intent of the author is only to offer information of a general nature to help you in your quest for emotional and spiritual well-being. In the event you use any of the information in this book for yourself, which is your constitutional right, the author and the publisher assume no responsibility for your actions.

Any people depicted in stock imagery provided by Getty Images are models, and such images are being used for illustrative purposes only. Certain stock imagery © Getty Images.

Print information available on the last page.

ISBN: 978-1-9822-5858-0 (sc)
ISBN: 978-1-9822-5859-7 (e)

Balboa Press rev. date: 02/05/2021

CONTENTS

PREFACE

Words have power. I first learned this concept as a young girl when my childhood best friend Tina and I would eagerly exchange notebooks on her front porch while other kids played hopscotch or tag in the street. Tina's notebook was filled with elaborate short stories, mainly inspired by the soap operas of the day. My notebook was filled with poems; sometimes silly and carefree, others filled with the romantic notions of a young girl. We couldn't wait to read what the other had written, and we were, without a doubt, each other's biggest fan.

The first time I learned that words can cause immense laughter was when, at the age of 10, I wrote a poem called Chitter, about a sweet little mouse who met with a devastating ending. When I read this poem to my parents one weeknight (they even turned off the TV to listen to me!), my Dad was so shocked at the ending of that story that he literally fell to his knees with laughter. He did not see that ending coming at all. Truth be told, they probably wanted to sign me up for therapy sessions after that!

I later learned that words can raise emotions that lead to tears. Not necessarily tears of sadness, but tears because the words touched someone's heart and invoked emotion. My brother came across a folder of my poems that I had typed up and stored on the family computer (long before the days of everyone in the family having their own laptops). He read "And As We Grew" one night without me knowing, and he told me later that as he read it, he realized the tears were flowing down his face.

Finally I learned that words can cause joy, in others and in myself, when I wrote my sister and brother-in-law's wedding invitation and saw my words in print for the first time, or a tribute to my friend's Dad for his 75th birthday. Or the way my Mom would always drop everything to listen to my newest poem. Obviously "A Mother's Love" was written for her.

Words have the power to move people to tears, or to feel joy, anger, love, or simply to reflect and remember. Some are written with youthful optimism, others are more jaded and cynical, which reflects this emotional roller coaster called life. I hope that no matter where you are in your life, something in this book touches your heart (well…hopefully not the anger part!).

DEDICATION

For my Dad, who was my first fan, and for my Mom, who (if she were here) could finally stop saying "I wish you would do something with your writing!"

The first poem that I would like to share actually has two versions. The original, below, was written several years ago. I have no issue with it, other than when I decided I wanted to read it at a friend's wedding, and did not think the maudlin ending was suitable for the happy occasion. So I revised the ending which is on the following page.

Both versions are written from the Bride's point of view to her Groom and both deal with respect. However in the first version, the Bride is only concerned about protecting her own heart. In retrospect, I have to wonder why she is marrying this person if she is so worried that her heart will get broken!

In the second version, she brings her Groom into it, realizing that love and respect is a two-way street and both people must work together to protect each other. This is a much better way to begin a marriage, don't you agree?

This Heart I Give
(Original Version)

It's a part of me, it's in my soul. Through the years I've felt it grow.
I hold it deep inside of me; I've never let it go.

But now there's you, my chosen one. I'm giving you my heart.
It holds the contents of my life. It's quite a work of art.

Take my heart and cherish it and hold it oh so tight.
It's precious and it's fragile and it must be treated right.

It's like a rose that's in full bloom when given proper care.
It's a gift I give with love to you, it's infinitely rare.

But like that rose that fades away if treated with neglect
You'll find my heart will wither too, if not treated with respect.

I vowed to love and honor you when I agreed to take your name;
To treat you daily with respect, from you I ask the same.

So keep in mind throughout your life, each day we both shall live,
The vow to honor and respect comes with this heart I give.

And if by chance some day you find this vow you must deny
My heart, like the neglected rose, will wither up and die.

This Heart I Give
(Revised Version)

It's a part of me, it's in my soul. Through the years I've felt it grow.
I hold it deep inside of me; I've never let it go.

But now there's you, my chosen one. I'm giving you my heart.
It holds the contents of my life. It's quite a work of art.

Take my heart and cherish it and hold it oh so tight.
It's precious and it's fragile and it must be treated right.

It's like a rose that's in full bloom when given proper care.
It's a gift I give with love to you, it's infinitely rare.

But like that rose that fades away if treated with neglect
You'll find my heart will wither too, if not treated with respect.

I vowed to love and honor you when I agreed to take your name;
To treat you daily with respect, from you I ask the same.

So keep in mind throughout your life, each day we both shall live,
The vow to honor and respect comes with this heart I give.

But love is not a one-way street, so I shall do my part
To also treat you with respect as I protect your heart.

And in this crazy world of ours love can get pushed aside;
Let's make a vow to not allow our feelings to subside.

And if that starts to happen, let's right now make a pact
To not only have each other's heart, but also each other's back.

As we start on this new journey – never more apart
Please know that when you take my hand, you also take my heart.

So please know this, from this day on, each day we both shall live
The Joy of spending life with you
Comes with this heart I give!

I wrote this for my Mom one Mother's Day many years back, but also as a tribute to all Mothers who sacrifice so much of themselves to care for their babies. I lost her in 2016 but I hope that she knew what an amazing Mom she was. Although I was never blessed with motherhood myself, I am a Mom to fur babies whom I love with all my heart, so I can only imagine the immense love a Mother must feel for her child.

A Mother's Love

Sometimes you cannot substitute
A mother's love and care.
You can't replace the tender touch
Or the smile that's always there.

How does she find the time to do
The things she needs to do,
And still have time left in her day
To give her love to you?

Where does she find the energy
To always give so much,
And let you lean your weight on her
As if she was a crutch?

No matter where you travel,
She's always in your sight
To lend a reassuring word
That things will be alright.

For long ago, inside her body
Your life had begun.
Although you are two people now,
Part of you will be one.

Long before you saw the world
She realized your worth,
And loved and cared and nurtured you
For months before your birth.

As infinite as sun and sky
And waves upon the sand,
Her love is there throughout your life
To lend a helping hand.

You cannot help but grasp the helping hand
That grasps your own.
You need that strength from time to time
Although you are full grown.

You thought you didn't need her
When you cut the apron string.
But still you need your mother's touch
To dry the tears that sting.

But never fear, her love is there
Come Hell or flooding waters.
For a mother tends to shower love
Upon her sons and daughters.

But a mother is a person too,
She needs love in return.
To NOT take her for granted
Is a lesson we must learn.

So tell your mother "Thank you",
It's not so hard to say.
To tell her that you love her
Is so small a price to pay.

It's with these words that I give thanks
And with these words I pray,
To do the best that I can do
To be like her someday!

Let's not forget our Dads who also sacrifice and are such a pillar of strength in our lives. This poem came to be when my friend Linda approached me to put together a tribute to her Dad for his 75th birthday. She told me how she was feeling and what she wanted to convey in her message. Her Dad was very devoted to the Church and the family would go to Church together each Sunday, something Linda was not too crazy about as she grew up, preferring to sleep in on those Sunday mornings. But as she got older, she too realized the strength that she gained from going to Church, and as her faith got stronger, she appreciated her Dad so much for making the Church such an important part of their lives. She wanted to make sure that point was conveyed to him.

When she read this, she got very emotional and thanked me for the words. I told her she was wrong to thank me. These were her words to her Dad, I just made them rhyme.

My Father, My Friend

My dad, my pal, my confidante
You're all that I could ever want
In a father and a friend
I cherish every day we spend
Together or just on the phone
With your voice near I'm not alone.
I know you'll always help me and
Guide me with your gentle hand.

Yet still you seem to realize
I don't see always through your eyes.
You listen to each word I say
(Like you could stop me anyway!).
Even when we'd disagree
You never turned your back on me.
When I stood my ground and would not budge
You never held a single grudge.

I hardly was the perfect child;
Never shy and rarely mild.
I'd often groan and make a fuss
When you would do what's right for us

Like taking us to Church and such,
And now you'll never know how much
I need that in so many ways
To get me through the trying days.

And now I seem to understand
Why you are so strong a man.
God's love, which was never far
Helped make you the man you are.

So Happy Birthday – Let us toast
To a man who means the most.
Let's celebrate and have some fun.
Way to go Dad, job well done!

Of course I have to include my Dad. Although he was not a religious person, he raised us with good values and a sense of responsibility. He would often lecture us when we displeased him, jabbing the tip of his index finger into our shoulder as he spoke. The family joke was, if we were ever in a plane crash, don't send for dental records; just look for the indentation in our shoulder. Seriously, that makes him sound like an ogre, but it was done with love as he only wanted us to be better people. And isn't that a parent's job? People used to tell me that I look just like him. I inherited his thick hair and his nose. The hair I am thrilled about, the nose..not so much.

This was written because he spent so much time in this place. This was his sanctuary; his man cave if you will. We always knew where to find him. After he passed suddenly in 1989, I used to stand in there and look around at all of the projects left unfinished and the personal objects he kept near and dear to him, and I felt closer to him somehow. This poem was a favorite of my Mom's, as she knew how much time her husband spent there.

His Garage

The tools lie dark and dusty
As they wait for skillful hands
To bring them all to life again
To dance with his commands.

Everything is peaceful,
Like the calm before the storm.
The hammer and the nails grow restless,
Anxious to perform.

This place was his palace
And in it he was king.
He could make those tools do a dance
Like puppets on a string.

In this place he spent his days
Doing what he loved best.
But now the show is over
And the actors are at rest.

A calendar upon the wall
Still marks that final year.
A box of broken watches lies still
Waiting for repair.

The dust has covered footprints
That once walked across the floor,
Enveloping them in their wake
Like waves upon the shore.

His friends that still reside here
Watch the days and seasons turn,
Growing anxious as they sit
Awaiting his return.

I pray that he is happy
In the place he now calls home.
His mind is free of all debris,
His spirit free to roam.

If there is a Heaven,
And I surely know there is,
For him I hope it is a place
That's similar to this.

For this place was his Heaven
Where his tensions would release,
And to know that he is happy
Puts me, like him, at peace.

This more recent work was inspired by the 2020 Covid-19 Quarantine. Many people, especially women, found themselves in the situation of having to deal with work responsibilities while learning the new task of home schooling. Some even had aging parents living with them, or young adults home early from colleges that shut down. More than once I was on a conference call where someone was trying to get lunch on the table for the kids or juggling work with online learning. I could hear the tension and sensed the distraction, but I knew they were doing their absolute best to hold it all together. Even though I can't say I empathize with them, as I am not in that same situation, I do sympathize with them, and they definitely have my respect.

In The Middle

Don't just live for the moment,
I heard somebody say.
Instead live for the moments
That take your breath away.

But life can get so busy
And time goes by so fast.
It's hard to embrace the present
When my thoughts live in the past.

For in the past when I was young
My life was so carefree.
Before the days of work and kids,
My life belonged to me.

How can I not go back there,
At least within my mind?
The task list just gets longer;
It's so hard to just unwind.

My boss hands me a deadline,
I'd better do it quick!
Oh no, not now! I hear a sneeze
I think my child's sick.

The other one is hungry
As I listen to his cries.
The phone, it won't stop ringing
As my stress intensifies.

The nursing home is calling.
Dad fell down again.
I know I have to get there
But I can't imagine when.

My husband wants some romance,
I just need some sleep.
I close my eyes, ignore his sighs
And pray that I don't weep.

I know I sound ungrateful.
That is not my intent.
But these days are just so hectic,
Every nerve is spent.

I know that I sound selfish,
And I know that I am blessed.
But in between this quarantine
There's so little time to rest.

The alarm goes off too early,
Time for another day.
I'll do my best to find those things
That take my breath away.

This poem is about the little boy/girl next door, and the bonds that last a lifetime. Although there were plenty of boys in the neighborhood that I crushed on, there was no one next door that I set my sights on. But I do love hearing stories of people who were lucky enough to find "the one" when they were barely out of diapers! My friend Trish's parents met when they were 4 years old and they just celebrated their 60th anniversary! Here's to them, and everyone who grew up with the love of their life!

And As We Grew

When I was just a little girl
With shining eyes of blue,
I looked upon the house next door
And somehow I just knew.

For in that house there was a boy
With dusty eyes of gray
Who made my heart dance in my throat
When he would glance my way.

But little boys don't waste their time
On girls and sweet romance.
Quite opposite, they'll run from them
If given half a chance.

But in this boy next door I sensed
A warm sincerity,
As if somehow I always knew
His path would lead to me.

And through the years as we both grew
My heart would swell with pride
When he would enter through a room
And I'd be by his side.

And as we grew I felt the yearning
All young girls must feel
When dealing with their changing lives
And pain that is quite real.

But through the adolescent years
And early college days,
We journeyed down two different paths
And went our separate ways.

From time to time I'd think of him;
The yearning would not end.
I'd count the days until I could see
My faithful, trusted friend.

When finally that day approached
I wasn't quite prepared
To come to terms with what I felt;
I really was quite scared.

For suddenly the boy next door
Had grown into a man
Who made my fingers turn to gel
When he would touch my hand.

And now I stand before him
In my wedding gown of white.
I see him walking toward me
And my heart sings with delight.

I say these vows with loving faith
Of what he means to me.
I put this ring upon my finger
For the world to see.

And as we grow and live our lives
Our two worlds become three.
And again a boy with dusty eyes
Has captivated me.

And as we watch him grow
I see that time is slipping fast.
We reminisce about our lives
And of days gone past.

And someday soon I know
We'll have to let each other go
To meet again in another place
Where once again we'll grow.

The child we raised together
Is now leading his own life.
We watched him grow from boy to man,
And now he takes a wife.

The memories roll down my cheeks
In tiny drops of tears
As I look through fading photographs
Of our younger years.

I realize, with silent pride,
As I look at my men
I'd live my life over again
If only just for them.

This is another poem inspired by recent events of our times. This is one of the moments in life where you will never forget where you were when you heard the news. While watching the towers fall, or the planes crashing into the Pentagon and the Pennsylvania field, you knew that precious lives were lost and those lives that remained here on Earth were changed forever. The quick cadence of this poem hopes to capture the ever changing emotions, confusion, and despair of that time. May we never forget.

09/11

When seconds count and moments matter
Life can change before your eyes.
Hearts will break and souls will shatter
And yet we do not realize

That life is short, it can be over
With neither blink nor second glance.
No one holds a four leaf clover
In this daily game of chance.

Cries of anger, cries of fear,
Drowning quickly in our grief.
Loneliness beyond repair
Searching blindly for relief.

Yet on and on our lives revolve
Another dollar, another day.
Another life left in despair,
Another soul taken away.

Another loved one, standing, staring,
Soul shattered, teary eyed.
Bruised and battered, heart strings tearing,
Anger overflows inside.

Ahh…there was a boy. How many stories start out like that? This poem is autobiographical. Many years ago I had a long distance telephone romance with one of my customers at work. He lived on the East coast and would call in daily with his order. We would talk about our weekend or upcoming plans, and then eventually he started asking for me when he called in. Conversation turned to flirting, and taking way too long on the calls, which my boss was none too happy about. Eventually we exchanged home phone numbers. We would talk on the phone every couple of nights for hours long into the dawn, driving our phone bills up into the hundreds of dollars, as this was before the days of cell phones and prepaid minutes, or Skype or Facetime. We had no idea what the other looked like. We did our best to describe ourselves to each other, but honestly that was such a small part of our connection, which was really based on emotions and not physicality. The feelings were growing very strong and we knew we had to meet, so finally he booked his flight. Well of course you can imagine my anticipation as I waited at the airport gate (this was before 09/11 when you could still go to the gate and wait for a flight or see someone off). When he finally got off the plane we embraced of course, but that was the extent of it. There was no chemistry at all! Without a phone in between us, we literally had nothing to say. It was so awkward, and to call it a letdown would be an understatement. We had a nice weekend regardless, but when I watched his plane take off on Sunday evening I felt a range of emotions from confusion, to disappointment, and finally contentment. Here is that story.

A Guy I Knew..

I watched you walk away from me
My fingers wave good-bye.
I see that jet plane carry you
Into the blackened sky.

I press my face against the pane,
An imprint marks my nose.
My tear-streaked face looks like the glass
Where condensation flows.

I wonder what you're thinking now.
Are your thoughts one big blur?
Don't you see, this trip was good.
We had to know for sure.

For all those months of waiting
And all those miles apart
Were weighing heavy on my mind
And damaging my heart.

We had to see this whole thing through,
Let nature take its course.
But we were like two magnets
Emitting the same force.

When we came too close together,
We quickly pushed away.
We were so much alike, it seemed,
We had nothing to say.

When you take a friendship
And try to make romance
You may end up with nothing,
There always is that chance.

But we were both so loving.
Our friendship was so warm.
I thought that we were strong enough
To weather any storm.

Yet sometimes things just don't work out,
And one thing I have found,
The ones you count on most in life
Can sometimes let you down.

If and when that happens,
There's not much you can say.
Just gather up your self-respect,
And proudly walk away.

Today I watched a sad movie,
The tears shed at its end.
I wanted to rewind that show
And play it once again.

I felt the same way that I felt
When I watched you walk away.
As if our lives were a movie
I wanted to replay.

For our story was one I would
Most certainly repeat.
The feelings were so special;
The memories, bittersweet.

I didn't feel hurt this time;
No gnawing, numbing pain.
I only saw the rainbow
But there wasn't any rain.

I felt relief flow through my veins.
I felt so young and free,
As if these past months I was blind
And once again could see.

I watched that jet plane carry you
Home where you belong.
Our hearts now know the answer
That our minds knew all along.

I feel a sense of calmness,
For along with dignity
I have another chance to find
The one who's right for me.

I don't recall the inspiration behind this next poem, but it continues on the theme of the previous poem, "A Guy I Knew", and dealing with heartache and disappointment, and ultimately how that makes us stronger. Life is going to be hard and full of pain, so we may as well get a lesson out of it, and perhaps relish the opportunity for some personal growth.

When you Hurt

Sometimes it's hard to understand
The way that things work out.
It's hard to keep your spirit light
When your head is full of doubt.

It's tough to know just who to trust
And who will let you down.
It's hard to wear a smile
When your heart just wants to frown.

You long for someone's tender touch
To wipe away a tear,
But you cry into your pillow
Because no one else is there.

And in the morning sunlight
You try so hard to smile
But in your heart you know the hurt
Is going to last awhile.

Eventually, you know the pain
Will gradually subside.
Still deep down you feel the anger
That you try so hard to hide.

You realize that life is strange
Yet still you question why.
But you'll never know the answers
Until the day you die.

So still you go on living,
Although part of you is not.
You struggle through each passing day
With all the strength you've got.

And someday soon you'll understand
When the sun clears up the rain,
Your spirit will be stronger
Because it felt the pain.

On a happier note, here is the wedding invitation written for my sister and brother-in law. It was thrilling to see my words in print for the first time and being mailed out to over 200 people! They are approaching their 30th anniversary next year, so I would like to hope I contributed to their happy ending!

Today I Give My Love

Today I give my love to him,
I've waited all my life
To stand before him proud and true
And become his faithful wife.

Today I give my love to her,
I've waited for so long
To take her hand inside of mine
And hold it proud and strong.

From this day forward I shall spend
A lifetime loving my best friend!

This is another one where I can't quite recall the inspiration behind it, but honestly the majority of what I write is not based on my own experiences. In this case it could have been based on a friend's heartbreak, or simply just inspired by watching flames dance in a fireplace. Inspiration comes from many places, sometimes in places you least expect it, and suddenly an idea grows and takes shape.

The Last Waltz

Sitting by the fireside
It's cold, lonely, dark outside.
I stare into the glowing flame,
I feel the chill and hear your name.

I didn't quite know what to do
When you told me we were through.
I begged and pleaded you to stay
I watched you turn and walk away.

I wonder, as I watch the fire,
How the one I most desire
Could say he loves me then with a sigh
Kiss my cheek and say good-bye?

I watch the flames that light the room
And contemplate impending gloom.
The flames, somehow they hypnotize
And dry the moisture from my eyes.

I cannot cry, the tears won't come.
My throat is dry, my body numb.
I speak your name and with a chill
I can't believe I'd want you still.

One by one the flames do die.
They do a dance, then say good-bye.
Much like you who danced before
You waltzed forever out my door.

The previous two poems mentioned that I cannot recall the inspiration behind them. This next one, aptly called <u>Inspiration</u>, deals with that question that I have received many times in my life "Where do you get your ideas?". I am sure many artists and authors are asked the same question. Honestly I don't know, and this poem sums that up. Sometimes an experience in life can spur inspiration, like my Father's death in "His Garage", or my long distance relationship in "A Guy I Knew", and what I learned from that experience. The more recent "In the Middle", inspired by the 2020 Quarantine started with just four words bouncing around my head while in the shower. By the time I got out of the shower, I had four verses written, and quickly ran with my towel wrapped around me to grab pen and paper. Oddly enough, only two of those four initial words made it into the poem. One of the later verses took hold in my mind while I was driving, and I had to pull over into a parking lot to quickly write it down. Lately I have taken advantage of modern technology, and have texted myself lines or versus if something pops into my head and I don't have pen or paper handy.

Sometimes it's events in other people's lives that cause the words to flow, as with my friend Linda asking me to write her words into a poem for her Dad in "My Father, My Friend", or my sister's wedding invitation.

My friend Trish's wedding to Mark is what inspired me to revise "This Heart I Give", to give it a more likeable ending to be read at a wedding and that is actually what motivated me to write this book. I had not written anything in a very long time, and honestly had not even thought of my writing in many years. This wasn't intentional. Life just got busy as I was working full time, pursuing a Master's Degree, and more recently taking on a supplemental career as a fitness instructor. In between all of that I was dealing with my Mother's illness and eventual death, and my niece's illness (thankfully she's fine now!). So any new writing or any previous works were definitely not on my mind. When the quarantine of 2020 happened, boredom hit and many of us looked for projects to fill the days. Mine was to clean up my front hall closet (which I never actually did) along with a file cabinet called my Memory Drawer, which was starting to sink into the drawer below it, it was so overstuffed. But in that drawer I found my old pink binder with all of my writings. As I started reading through some of them, I thought about how my Mother always wanted me to do something with my writing, and how she would have loved it if I had been more open with my work. I started thinking of my own death (morbid, I know) and how these poems would die with me, so an idea brewed. I was going to share my book of poems with my best friend's Helene and Trish and tell them that if anything happened to me, to please place these poems all around the funeral home during my wake, the way that most people post pictures. Well then I thought, that's really not fair to put that burden onto them, so it spurred me to finally get off my tush and "do something with my writing". The third verse of this poem, which was written in June of 1991, deals with this concern.

Inspiration

I hear a voice inside my head,
The words go round and round.
I quickly reach for pad and pen
And rush to write it down.

I cannot explain from where I get
This wandering melody.
It comes from a forceful inner voice
So deep inside of me.

It's as if this voice inside of me
Has so much more to say
To leave my mark upon the world,
For I'll be gone someday.

And if my words live on and on
And touch one person's soul,
Or bring a smile to just one face
Then I've achieved my goal!

This next poem gets a little preachy, in my opinion, but the message is definitely one that is needed in these current, turbulent times. This writing has to do with getting worn down from the inside out, and how that can translate to our exterior, and how we deal with life and other people. Just today I had to talk to a friend who was having a hard time dealing with all of the negativity and verbal word wars on social media, especially as this is an election year. All of this fighting was stealing her joy and tarnishing her from the inside out. She has so many good and positive things going on in her life and this is wearing her down. As I told her, we cannot control what is going on in the world or how people are reacting to it. All we can do is control our own actions and that may include taking a break from social media, and/or shutting off the TV for awhile until things in the nation calm down a little. That doesn't mean being ignorant to current events or what is happening outside our homes, but there has to be that balance between controlling what you can, and letting the stuff you cannot control go. Otherwise it will start to have an impact on all areas of your life. It's like the airline tells you right before the flight takes off; "put your own oxygen mask on first". It is only then that you can be strong enough to take care of other people.

Inner Beauty

I did not grow up well-to-do,
I did not grow up poor.
I certainly wasn't beautiful
Nor ugly to the core.

I had few clothes that were all mine;
Mostly hand-me-downs.
I'd wander through the clothes-filled stores,
My face would wear a frown.

I found the more that I grew up
The more I longed to be
The kind of girl that made boys take
A second glance at me.

How foolish was I in my youth?
So concerned with vanity,
When the real beauty in myself
Lie deep inside of me.

All that time as I grew up
Spent in front of mirrors.
I never thought of how my spirit
Had tarnished through the years.

Anger and frustration
Can sometimes take its toll.
So I make it part of my routine
To daily cleanse my soul.

I clean out all the demons
That gather through the day.
I sweep away the dustiness
That turns my spirit gray.

In the morning when I wake
I have a fresh new start
Because I swept away the dirt
That gathered on my heart.

I recommend you do the same
To keep your spirit clean.
Make grooming of your inner self
A part of your routine.

Because others may not notice
That you're clean from head to toe.
But when you clean your inner self
You cannot hide the glow.

For outer beauty has its flaws
That we've all learned to hide.
But you can't conceal the beauty
When you feel so good inside!

As I mentioned earlier, it is 2020 in America and a month before a Presidential election. I have seen friendships destroyed and families take very strong stands over differences of opinion, choices of candidates, and freedoms at risk.

If that is not chaotic enough, add in the civil unrest and things in this country have become very tumultuous. There have been protests and riots and looting; tearing down of statues and those who want to destroy our history. It is a very scary time and I have never seen such unrest in my lifetime. Our amazing Military is stationed all over the world fighting for us and our freedoms including (as I have been reminded) our right to protest, and to take a knee. I know that America has a long history, and this too shall pass. Our country is not perfect, nor has it had an uncheckered past. All that I can hope for is that our country learns from past mistakes and strives to do better.

Have you ever had a friend or family member, maybe a child, do something that you disagreed with, or watched them go down the wrong path? You probably had some anxiety or unrest as you watched mistakes being made, and you probably feared for their safety but you knew that these mistakes were inevitable as you hoped they would learn from them, and grow stronger. Maybe you hoped daily that this would be the day things would turn around. Hopefully they did, but maybe they did not, and if so I would bet you still kept loving them regardless, and praying for them and their safety. That is how I feel about America. I may not always agree with how things are. I may want better for our country and for our future. I do fear for its safety and the safety of all of us. But I will always love it, and I will always fight for it, flaws and all.

Dear America

Our country is in turmoil.
Our country's in despair.
What's happening to America?
There's chaos everywhere.

I cannot help but wonder
Where did we take this turn?
When did it become acceptable
To let Old Glory burn?

I can't help but grow anxious
As monuments are defaced;
Old statues being ripped right down -
Our history erased.

Millions of men and women
Are so far from home, deployed.
To honor them, it's hard to watch
Our country be destroyed.

Yet they are fighting for just this,
So we can all be free
And that people who make millions
Can so proudly take a knee.

I do respect those who take a stand
To get their voices heard.
But is rioting and looting
The best way to spread your word?

The pulling down of statues
Was met with great applause.
But I'm confused on how destruction
Helps in furthering your cause.

America, it has its flaws,
On that we can agree.
But as you fight for freedoms dear to you
Don't take mine from me.

My Dad and Grandpa went to war.
I wonder what they'd say
If they saw the state that it's in now;
Their beloved USA.

Flaws and all, to me it is
The best country in the land.
So while people choose to take a knee,
I choose to proudly stand.

I feel a chill as I watch Old Glory
Wave red, white, and blue.
I love you – Dear America,
I'll always stand for you.

We are currently in the fall season, and I have my Vanilla Pumpkin candle burning and all of my scarecrows and Halloween decorations out. The evenings are getting darker earlier and there is a definite chill in the air. I enjoy all of these things, but I live for summertime, which is just a mere 3 months and then it is gone. I know winter is right around the corner and I am not too thrilled about that, but the Earth keeps revolving, and eventually it will be summer and a joyous 85 degrees again! But first…Spring!

It's Springtime Once Again!

I hear a bird outside my window
Singing me a song.
The trees are dancing with new leaves,
The flowers dance along.

The grass gives way to brilliant green
And overtakes the white.
The lovers walk through wooded parks;
The stars shine with delight.

I feel like an intruder
As I open up the door.
The sun has crept through parted blinds
And makes love to the floor.

I feel it in my heart and soul
That spring is in the air.
I whistle an uplifting tune,
The breeze blows back my hair.

Yes! Mother Earth has woken up
From her winter's nap.
She takes the world by the hand
And holds it in her lap.

She wipes the slumber from her eyes
And steps out of her bed.
She kicks away the winter clouds
And brings spring rain instead.

I watch the chipmunks playing tag
Up the blooming trees.
I wonder what the babbling brook
Is saying to the breeze.

I hear the children's laughing voices
As they fly a kite.
Up up higher, there it goes!
They'd better hold on tight!

I feel so calm and peaceful
As I look over this land,
As if the earth and I are one
Walking hand in hand.

Then all at once it dawns on me
How much I love this earth.
The world has been reborn today;
Let's celebrate the birth!

When my Father died suddenly during his sleep on a cold night in October, 1989, our family was understandably shocked and devastated. In order to comfort us, and when things died down a bit, my Parent's best friends purchased a star in my Dad's name to honor him. So I have to believe the inspiration for this next poem came from that. Many years later, my Mom passed away after several months in the hospital. Even though we had time to prepare and spend time with her right up until the end, we were still understandably heartbroken. That led me to question which is easier to bear; losing someone suddenly where your world is rocked because you did not see it coming, or watching someone slowly fade away over a period of time. The answer, I can assure you, is neither. They both come with their own sets of regrets and what-if's. And at the end of each situation, the result is the same; they are gone and you are left behind to carry on in whatever way you can.

So do I think my Dad is that star in the sky? No. But do I think there is something out there that helps to guide us? Yes, I do believe that. I have felt it more than once, countless times even. I am not sure if it is my Dad or Mom, or perhaps another relative (I am the spitting image of my Grandmother Ida, who I never met, but always felt a strong connection to her), but I have felt a strength that I cannot deny feeling. Sometimes it was during times of struggle when I needed some encouragement, other times it was just random and seemed to come out of nowhere. But something was there. Do you believe? Maybe or maybe not, or perhaps you want to but still remain a little skeptical, and I understand that. But for me, in this crazy world with so many challenges that we face daily, does it hurt to hold out a little hope that something may exist to guide us along?

So Long For Now

I looked into the midnight sky,
Not sure what I would find.
I saw a star that winked at me,
Or was it in my mind?

I looked again just to be sure,
Was I really sane?
Or was it only wishful thinking
To help me ease my pain?

No. It was something more I felt.
The feeling was too strong.
This star was reaching for my hand
And guiding me along.

I put my hand inside of it
And let it lead the way.
Instantly I felt inside
That things would be okay.

Then suddenly it dawned on me,
This was my guiding light
To help me through each passing day
And every lonely night.

This strength felt so familiar,
Like someone very dear.
It couldn't be – I shook my head,
And wiped away a tear.

Then I began to wonder
What happens when we die?
Do we become the midnight stars
That glisten in the sky?

Will we someday be guiding lights
That twinkle from above;
External lights that shine so bright
Upon those that we love?

To know that those I've loved and lost
Found a peaceful place to go
Brings some Heaven down to Earth
And helps me to let go.

So now when I find troubled times
I look into the sky,
And I feel that helping hand reach out
With a strength I can't deny.

And all at once I know inside
That things will be alright.
So long for now, my little star
For I'll see you tonight.

Continuing on the theme of loss, I remember I was very young, in my early teens, when I wrote this next poem. Even though it sounds like it was written for a person, I believe I wrote this after my little puppy Samantha died. She had been a birthday gift when I turned 14, and I had an instant bond with her; this floppy haired little brown Lhasa apso. I remember she would sit on the edge of the bathtub when I'd take a bath, and dip her paw into the bath water. She and I did everything together. When she was old enough to be spayed, we took her in that morning for the routine procedure. But unbeknownst to us, little Samantha had a heart problem and died of heart failure on the operating table. I remember getting off the school bus and seeing my Mom's car in the driveway and running into the house looking for my little friend, but finding my Mom, who had to deliver the horrible news. My family, even my Dad, cried all that night and for days after. This was the first time I felt the incredible bond and unfortunate loss of a beloved pet, especially one this young. I am sorry to say that I have felt that loss many times over as I have gotten older and rescued several animals from shelters, some of them already several years old when I adopted them. Either way, whether they are babies or adults when you bring them into your life, they are not with us nearly long enough. We really only borrow them for a short time. Each time I have to say goodbye, my heart shattering, I vow I will never subject myself to that heartbreak again. But I'm sure you can guess, someone always follows me home and once again I let them into my heart. And quite honestly, I would not want to live without them. The joy they give in the days that you have them far surpasses the sorrow when they leave.

My eyes began to water
And the tears began to flow.
My heart began to sink,
And everything felt low.

I know my problems won't be solved
If I sit here and cry.
But you just meant so much to me,
Why did you have to die?

I know that crying about you
Won't bring you back here.
But you and I were always together;
An inseparable pair.

You brought me so much happiness,
But now that will all erase.
I think of fond memories
And I see your smiling face.

You made me laugh when I was sad.
Your touching words made me cry.
I was so proud to be with you,
Why did you have to die?

Christmas was always a big deal in my house growing up. We didn't get much in the way of new clothes or toys throughout the year unless we really needed something, but my parents more than made up for it on Christmas morning. I remember lying in bed early on December 25th and I could see the Christmas tree lit up. I would lie there with anticipation of all the goodies that awaited us, until finally at 5:00am my sister Sue would come and wake everyone up. That's funny to me now, because these days she's known to lie in bed until noon on the weekends! Christmas morning, and the entire holiday season are some of my best memories. But it is not like that for everyone, and despite the bright lights and festive music, it can be a very lonely and trying time for many people. Our own Christmases have drastically changed over the years. Both parents are gone, and my brother and his family recently moved several states away. So it is up to Sue and me now to carry on the traditions of the season. We do our best, but it is not the same, nor should we expect that it would be. Now that our holiday is so downsized, we always include people that we know do not have any where to go to celebrate. We should have been doing that all along, but people and families can sometimes get caught up in their own traditions and we forget about others that may have no family or a place to go.

This next poem was written for dear friend of mine, someone I love very much, who was going through a hard time at the holidays and wasn't up for celebrating the joys of the season. I hope these words helped.

A Not So Merry Christmas

I know that these are troubling times
And you don't feel so great.
And even though it's Christmas time
You cannot celebrate.

For sometimes life has funny ways
Of turning upside down.
I hope it brings you comfort
Just to know that I'm around.

Please know that I am here for you
Standing by your side,
Helping you to stand up tall
And face the world with pride.

I've known you for so many years
And I have watched you grow
Into the kind of person that
I am honored to know.

So keep in mind this Christmas
As you're gathered 'round the tree
My thoughts are with you always
Even though I cannot be.

Throughout this troubled Christmas
When your thoughts are sad and blue,
I hope knowing that I'm here for you
Will help you make it through.

These next three poems were written when I was very young, maybe 15 or 16. I didn't have a serious beau at that age and had not experienced any broken hearts (yet) so I am sure these are not about me or my experiences. Reading them back, I can see the common theme of lost love and looking back on a romance, rehashing the good memories. All of them have quite a bit of drama and romance, but what is unsettling to me now many years later, is the desperation in the narrative, especially in the first of the three, "Seems Like Only Yesterday". The fact that the person says that their life was empty and meaningless without another person is troubling to me now. In the second one, "I Never Sang Alone", the person states that all their misery would disappear if the person came back. And in the third one, "Remember When", the person gets their dream ending because the person came back to them, but also states that they would die if the person left them again. However it has a much more whimsical tone, and really, who doesn't enjoy a happy ending?

I am glad that I have gotten to a point in my life where I don't rely on other people for my happiness, nor do I feel that if someone leaves me, my life will be over. I have experienced loss in many forms, and life does indeed go on. My life would be different, of course, and I would most definitely miss the person and spend some time reflecting on memories, both happy and sad (probably with one or two glasses of Pinot Grigio and a box of tissues!). That's normal human behavior. But I think that learning to be happy and comfortable in your own skin is a hard lesson for many to learn. I hope that you have found that inner peace, because it does bring a certain amount of confidence and strength to know that you can stand on your own two feet in this world.

Seems like Only Yesterday

Sometimes it seems like yesterday
since you last left my heart.
Other times it seems like forever
Since we've been apart.

I always wonder why you left
When we had so much at stake.
Please say you'll try to understand;
I've had all that I can take.

Your memory fills up my mind
Until I can't take another minute.
My life is empty, meaningless,
Without you somewhere in it.

Although we tried to work it out,
Things got in the way.
The good times that we shared
Seem like only yesterday.

Seems like only yesterday
We romped through virgin snow.
And with all our might we conquered heights
No one else will ever know.

Seems like only yesterday
We chased a silk winged butterfly,
And stood and watched the sun
Create a mirage across the sky.

Although sometimes it hurts
To think of you and all we had,
I remember the best of times
And I know it's not so bad.

Now it's time to realize
That you're forever gone,
And I should have the strength and courage
To want to carry on.

I know sometimes it's going to hurt
When I begin to think of you.
But I'll always have our memories
To help to pull me through.

I want those memories always with me.
I want them to forever stay.
They remind me of the good times,
That seem like only yesterday.

I Never Sang Alone

The flowers in the garden
All bow their heads and moan
As I walk through the garden
Singing all alone.
I have no one to sing with,
For no one else is there.
Well I never sang alone when you were near.

The word "love" has no meaning
Now that you are gone.
I have no one to laugh with
Or no one to share my song.
We used to sit beneath the moon,
Just you and me,
And together we would sing a tune
In perfect harmony.
I try to put meaning into my songs
But the words come out unclear.
Well I never sang alone when you were near.

You left me oh so quickly;
In a flash you were gone.
You ended a perfect romance
And you ended a perfect song.
But all my misery would go away
If you'd just reappear,
For I never sang alone when you were near.

Remember When

Sitting in the sun in the middle of July
I've got you on my mind once again.
Thinking of the love we shared,
Of all those times you said you cared,
I wonder if you still remember when.

Remember when birds used to fly
And sing to us a lull-a-bye
And we would always join in with a song?
The trees above us would bow and dance
As if they shared in our romance,
And sometimes they would even sing along.

But I thought no one could ever be
More in love than you and me,
I thought our love would forever stay.
You said we were a fairy tale;
A love that never would grow stale;
That's why it hurt so when you went away.

Yet I saw you the other day.
You smiled as you glanced my way
But I just turned my gaze upon the floor.
You said that there just may be
Another chance for you and me,
You said you need me more than you did before.

But I turned my head, I was too proud
To let you hear me cry out loud.
I didn't want you to think I needed you.
But I felt myself begin to cry
So I turned and faced you with a sigh
And said I need you more than ever, too.

So somewhere in my heart I find
A love I thought I'd left behind
Is still there waiting for me once again.
And in spite of all my pride
Somewhere very deep inside
I want to revive the love that has once been.

The birds now once again do fly
And sing to us a lull-a-bye
As we join in singing a cheerful song.
The trees above us bow and dance
As if they share in our romance,
And they begin to also sing along.

No one else will ever be
More in love than you and me,
I know I've said it many times before.
But I mean it now, I think I'd die
Before I'd let you slip on by
You know I will be yours forevermore.

These next two I was even younger, probably 13 or so. These are both very short but still continue on the theme of romance and the other person being the center of the universe, but with a much more upbeat tone. I cringe a little when I read them but I wanted to include them because maybe the crazy world right now needs a little more love and romance!

You Are the One

Your eyes are as soft
As the ocean is blue.
Your lips are as moist
As the morning's fresh dew.

Your kiss is as warm
As the rays of the sun.
And I can tell by your smile
That you are the one!

You are the one
Who can wipe away sorrow
And give me all hope
For a brighter tomorrow.

You are the one,
With your special ways
Can capture some sunshine
To brighten my days.

You are the one,
Is true love like this?
You take me to Heaven
With one single kiss.

When I am cold
You warm me like the sun.
You are my sunshine;
You are the one!

If Ever a Man There Was

If ever a man could steal my heart
Make me long for his kindness when we are apart
Let me drown in his laughter and cry in his arms
Enchant me by turning on his special charms
One man can do these things like nobody does;
If ever a man there was.

If ever a man could fulfill all my hours
Lead me through gardens of bushes and flowers
Understand me when words are not even spoken
Fix anything – even my heart when it's broken
Share all of my dreams and protect all my cares
Put to rest all my worries and dry all my tears
One man does these things like nobody does;
If ever a man there was.

This poem is last, but it was also one of the first. Please keep in mind as you read this that I was 10 years old when I wrote it! So please forgive me for the tragic ending. I was probably just searching for words that rhymed together, and the story unfolded from there. As I mentioned in the beginning of this book, my parents probably considered sending me to therapy! Seriously though, I am a HUGE animal lover (I swerve for squirrels!) and would never advocate hurting an animal in any way. So I hope as you read this, you keep in mind the innocence in which it was written.

When I read this poem to my parents one weeknight, they listened intently with polite little smiles giving me courage to continue. But when I got to the part about Chitter's tragic demise, my Dad's eyes got as wide as saucers, and he literally fell down from the edge of his chair onto his knees, and roared with laughter! My mom and I started laughing at him laughing, and pretty soon I couldn't even finish the story. They definitely were NOT expecting that ending! The three of us sat there laughing for the longest time and later that night I could still hear my Dad laughing about it as I got ready for bed. It is definitely one of my fondest childhood memories, even if it did involve a dead mouse!

Chitter

Chitter was a little mouse
Who lived inside the Joneses house.
She found it very annoying that
She was never bothered by the cat.

She wanted the cat to notice her
But the little cat just wouldn't stir.
All Chitter wanted to do was play,
But Frisky, the cat, just slept all day.

So Chitter went back to her home,
Sat by her mirror and took out a comb
She sat and brushed her short gray fur
When an idea suddenly occurred to her.

Chitter finally decided that she was able
To take the long walk to the kitchen table.
She went to the table and dragged back a trap
Making sure that it didn't snap.

She reached the cat and without fail
Set the trap down by his long black tail.
Soon the mouse trap would be snapping
On the tail of the cat who was so lazily napping.

Chitter watched with a guilty feeling.
She wondered if this was as bad as stealing.
That reminded her of something, and quite pleased
She went to the freezer and stole some cheese.

She dropped the cheese into the trap
And watched in suspense until it snapped.
She was quite pleased with herself in that
She finally awoke the lazy cat.

But the cat did something that surprised Chitter,
He turned around and HE BIT HER!
He sunk his teeth into her head
And poor little Chitter was as good as dead.

Now Chitter, the monstrous little mouse
Lies buried under the Joneses house.
Memories of her are preserved
Though she finally got what she deserved.

AFTERWORD

What is in a name? That is a harder question than I ever thought! I've read hundreds if not thousands of books, and never really gave much thought into how the title came to be. Sometimes it was obvious, based around a main character or theme in the book. So when it came time to put a name to this book, I drew a blank, as my poems deal with many different themes and variations. Then when thumbing through my many creative writing notebooks from when I was very young, probably one that I shared with my childhood BFF Tina, I saw that I had called one of them "Walk through a Field of Flowers". Well it sounds lovely, and who doesn't want to walk through a plush garden? But what did it mean to me as a young child, and what does it mean to me now? I'm no philosopher; I never claimed to be. I am just exploring the innocent views of a child as compared to a somewhat jaded, sometimes cynical adult who has seen that life can be cruel at times, wonderful at others, turbulent and uncertain, and then calm and peaceful where everything seems to sigh and fall into place. I would imagine, going back to that time when I was 9 or 10 years old, I saw the world with great optimism, a vast garden to be explored. Today, I see broken or bent over stems weighed down when they should be standing tall and proud. I see beautiful roses bearing their prickly sides more often than their vibrant leaves, and I see the constant need for more…more water, more sunlight, more material possessions. But I also do see that beautiful garden, with many paths to be taken and so many gorgeous colors and shapes and sizes, each unique and special in its own way, and each with its own contribution to make in this world. And that gives me hope.

So how does life compare to this field of flowers? Here are some things I've learned.

People, like flowers, can die suddenly catching you totally by surprise, or slowly fade away, wilting a little more with each day. When you look back, you try to imagine what you could have done different or better. What signs did you miss that this demise was imminent? Was the flower starting to wilt a little under the pressure and were you just too busy to notice? Did this person show signs of being ill despite looking strong and sturdy? Was there anything you could have done to prolong this? Could you have given a little more of yourself to have prevented this from happening; perhaps a little more water, more time, love and attention? The hard truth is, despite our best efforts to will them to live, everything and everyone will die eventually and this is not our fault. I suppose a lesson we could take from that is that each departure from this world leaves room for new birth, new growth, and new opportunities.

Some flowers, like people, can light up the world with their beauty! Imagine a sunflower with its face open to the sky. It makes you smile every time, right? But even the beautiful rose comes with a prickly side and you have to be careful or it will make you bleed. Think about Hemlock. It may look harmless, but is very deadly to humans. Or the all too common Poison Ivy which comes with a warning label: "Leaves of three, let them be". Perhaps some people should come with such a warning label, because people can be toxic in our life too, and sometimes we have to feel the burn and itch before we realize it has happened. Right now, in our current situation in America, we are one month away from the 2020 election and I have never seen such division in our country, and such hatred spewed out on social media. I am not trying to get political, so I am stepping away right now from that topic, but the thing to remember is that people who are not serving you well are not serving you at all, and sometimes the best thing to do is run hard and fast away from them just like you would with that Poison Ivy. Do not allow people to poison you with their drama. We can be there for friends and family, of course. I am not saying we have to turn our backs on people who are struggling or in need of our help. But sometimes, if the drama starts to become toxic to us in our own lives and starts to impact our relationships with other important people in our lives, and if the other person is seeming to feed off that drama and draw you further in, we may have to carefully step out of that dark path and onto a greener passage.

Lastly, I'd like to borrow a verse from my favorite band Rush, in their final song called "The Garden", on their final album Clockwork Angels:

"The measure of a life is a measure of love and
respect, so hard to earn, so easily burned.
In the fullness of time A garden to nurture
and protect. It's a measure of a life".
* Songwriters: Geddy Lee / Alex Lifeson / Neil Elwood Peart

This song, to me, has to do with tending to our relationships as we would tend to our gardens, or our flowers. If you neglect either, you won't have to worry about them anymore, because time will take care of them for you.

I hope that as you walk through your field of flowers, you notice the beauty more than the dirt and worn paths; the colors and vibrancy more than the shadows; and I hope you take time to smell the roses...but watch out for those pricks!

With Deepest Gratitude…

To you, the reader, for taking the time to read this book. I know poetry can be difficult to get through and sometimes we just "don't get it", right? But I sincerely hope you found something here that you can relate to or something that made you smile, or perhaps shed a tear. If you allowed me into your precious time, and I touched your heart in any way, I am forever grateful.

To Tony, for your never ending support with not only this project, but everything in life that I take on. I know you have my back and you are always my protector and my best friend!

To my Brother Steve, who stumbled across my folder of poems one night and read them with the viewpoint of a young man, and liked them anyway! You became one of my earliest fans and I'll always appreciate how you had some of my poems printed and framed in your Bachelor pad! And thanks to my sister-in-law Doreen, who later allowed my work to be displayed in their new home.

To my Sister Sue, another one who, like our Mom, would say that she wished I would do something with my work. Well here you go. I just wish our Mom had seen this, but something tells me she knows. And thank you to my brother-in-law Dan, for allowing me to invite people to their wedding with my first printed invitation!

To my Stepdad Tim, who loved my Mom, and therefore us, unconditionally. You are a blessing to our family. And thank you for letting my work be displayed around yours and Mom's home.

To my niece's Kayley and Carson, and my Nephew Chase. Watching you all take the world by storm as you make your way gives me tremendous joy! I'm so proud of you! I love you all!

To Helene, my "oldest" (yeah I know you're younger than me!) best friend. Even though we don't see each other often I know you are there in a heartbeat if I need something, and back at ya! Your logic and common sense always reels me back in!

To Trish, my "newest" best friend, Louise to my Thelma! A 500 page book could not begin to include all of the fun, laughter, and adventures we've had over the past 4 years! And to Mark, whose love for you, and your upcoming wedding, inspired me to write again!

To Linda, whose beautiful words to your Dad live in my heart (I'm not crying, you're crying!), and to Janice, whose strength and kindness is an inspiration to me.

To Marian, even though it's been a lifetime, you were one of my earliest mentors, always eager to hear my latest work. I recently came across several clippings that you had sent to me years ago for poetry contests, and I thank you for your encouragement! I hope life finds you well!

To all of my friends, I am blessed with too many to mention you all, who always make life so much more interesting (especially when wine is involved!) I know will support me 100% in this, even if you may be slightly mad that I kept it a secret. But it was a good secret, right?

And lastly to Keith…who knew??

ABOUT THE AUTHOR

Kristin first began rhyming words together at a very young age, and soon these words expanded into poems and stories that enchanted family and friends. Creative Writing and English were her favorite classes. Once aspiring to hold a career writing greeting cards, life took Kristin on a different path into the business world, where she currently works for a communications company. Always an eager student, Kristin worked full time while earning her Bachelor of Science in Business Management degree, and later went on to earn her Master of Business Administration Degree from the University of Phoenix. It was during this time when her passion for writing took a back seat. Recently Kristin has explored her love of the fitness world by becoming a Certified Personal Trainer and Certified Pilates Instructor where she teaches several classes per week. Kristin is a huge animal lover and has volunteered for rescue organizations, many times bringing her "work" home with her in the form of a new furry friend. Kristin enjoys taking long rides in her convertible in the summer, and hitting some snow drifts in her Jeep in the winter. Kristin's favorite hobby is reading and she sometimes has five or six books going at one time (So many books…so little time!). This is her first book.

Printed in the United States
By Bookmasters